A Family in England

Copyright © 1988 by Lerner Publications Company

Map on pages 4-5 by J. Michael Roy. Back cover photograph
by Adrian Harvey. Photographs on pages 16 and 17 courtesy of
Hicri Koroglu.

LIBRARY OF CONGRESS CATALOGING-IN-PUBLICATION DATA

St. John, Jetty.
A family in England.

Summary: Describes the home, school, amusements, customs,
and work of a thirteen-year-old boy and his family living in a
small village near Cambridge.

1. England—Social life and customs—20th century—Juvenile
literature. 2. Family—England—Juvenile literature. [1.Family
life—England. 2. England—Social life and customs] I. Harvey,
Nigel, ill. II. Title.
DA589.4.S7 1988   942.082   87-35289
ISBN 0-8225-1679-9 (lib. bdg.)

Manufactured in the United States of America

1 2 3 4 5 6 7 8 9 10 98 97 96 95 94 93 92 91 90 89 88

A Family in England

Jetty St. John

Photographs by Nigel Harvey

Lerner Publications Company · Minneapolis

Peter McKee is 13 years old. He lives in Steeple Mordern, a small village a short drive from Cambridge in the southeast of England. Most people in England live in cities. England has been a leading manufacturing country since the 1700s.

England is part of the British Isles. It is the southern part of the island called Great Britain. Four countries—England, Scotland, Wales, and Northern Ireland—make up the United Kingdom of Great Britain and Northern Ireland. That's why England is sometimes referred to as "Great Britain," "Britain," or the "United Kingdom."

In the north of England is a ridge of mountains that continues into Scotland. The Midlands in the center of England are flatter and are traditionally linked with coal mining and industry. In the southwest of England there are small farms, open stretches of grassland, and a coastline of coves and beaches.

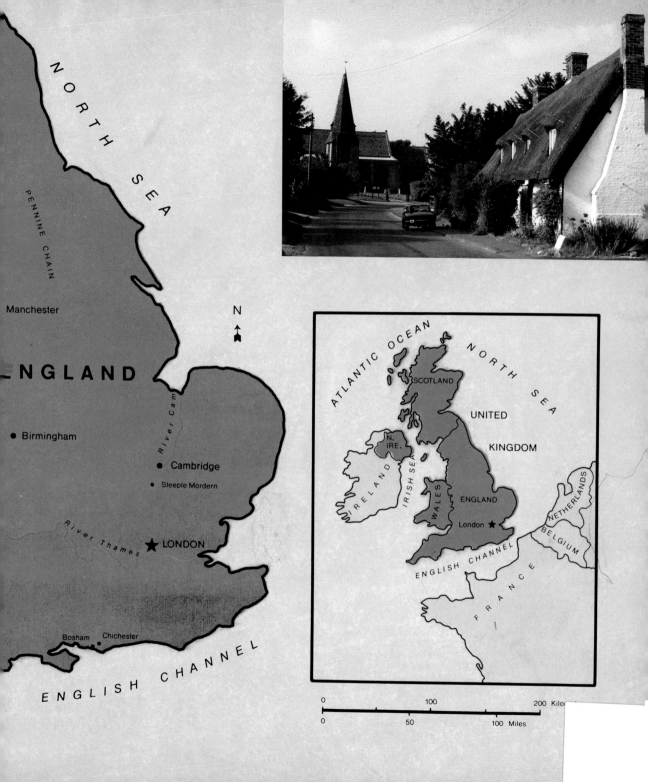

NORTH SEA

PENNINE CHAIN

Manchester

N

ENGLAND

Birmingham

River Cam

● Cambridge

● Steeple Mordern

River Thames

★ LONDON

Bosham Chichester

ENGLISH CHANNEL

ATLANTIC OCEAN

NORTH SEA

SCOTLAND

UNITED

KINGDOM

N. IRE.

IRELAND

IRISH SEA

WALES

ENGLAND

London ★

NETHERLANDS

BELGIUM

ENGLISH CHANNEL

FRANCE

| 0 | | 100 | | 200 Kilom |
| 0 | 50 | | 100 Miles | |

Peter has two brothers. Alastair is 15 and Thomas is 7. The family has a large fruit and vegetable garden, and in the summer the boys often pick raspberries to eat with cream. The lawn is kept short and the surface is flattened with a roller so it is in good shape for playing croquet.

Peter and Thomas both go to a school that prepares pupils so they can pass difficult entrance exams to get into a private high school. Children attend these "prep schools" from the ages of 4 to 13.

In England, private schools are called "public schools." Parents who send their children to "public schools" must pay school fees. Some schools, like Eton and Harrow, are very prestigious. To get in, children have their names placed on a waiting list from the moment they are born. Alastair, like most children in England, has always gone to a state school, which is free. Alastair tells Peter that if he wants to go to a public school he must speak upper-class English.

Mr. McKee is a timber broker. Every day he drives to his office in a town just north of London. He trades timber which is imported from Malaysia, New Zealand, North America, and Scandinavia. He then sells the wood in Europe. Most of the time Mr. McKee works in his office, but sometimes he flies to other countries to look at supplies of wood and to sign contracts.

While the boys are at school, Mrs. McKee works part time for a justice of the peace in a nearby town. She types out summonses which tell people to come to court. Often the documents are long and are written in formal legal language. One day she typed a summons for a person to come to court because he had abandoned a car in the ditch, and another one for a person who had stolen a pork pie.

In her spare time Mrs. McKee loves to work in the garden. It produces more fruit than the family can use, so she makes jam. She also bottles or cans vegetables such as beans and carrots.

This is Peter's last year at his prep school. He passed his common entrance exams in June, so he'll be able to go to a private school next year. His best subject is history. This year he won a book as the class prize in history, because his grades were so good. He also got a silver cup for being sportsman of the year. Peter goes to an all-boys school.

During the school's Speech Day the boys have swimming races and gymnastics in the morning while their families watch. Then they all eat a picnic lunch before the prizes are given out. The *headmaster*, or principal, hands out the trophies. The winners are congratulated, then there are lots of speeches, followed by afternoon tea.

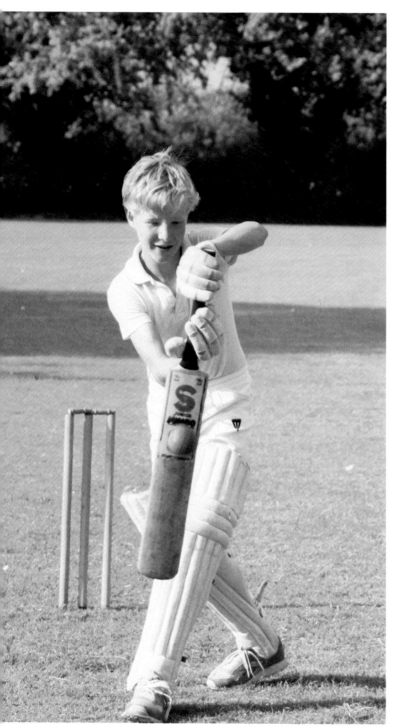

Cricket is Peter's favorite sport. Almost every town and village in England has a cricket *pitch* —the field where the game is played. During the summer, teams play in the evenings or on Saturday afternoons. Cricket is played with a bat and ball. The players divide into two teams. They try to score runs and protect their *wickets*, stumps of wood in the ground. Cricket looks a little like baseball, but it is very different. Cricket matches are usually formal affairs, and the rules have not changed much in almost 700 years. For comfort, many spectators bring blankets and folding chairs. Peter plays on his school cricket team, and sometimes they play against the village team.

In the summer the McKees enjoy going to Cambridge for an evening on the River Cam. They rent a shallow boat, called a punt. A long pole is used to push the punt along. Mr. McKee says he would do it, but the last two times he tried, the pole got stuck in the bottom of the river, and he fell in.

Matthew, the oarsman, is a student at Cambridge University, one of the best known universities in the world. Cambridge is divided into many colleges. The grounds of one of the colleges, St. John's, run down to the river. Much of the architecture at Cambridge is famous. Matthew explains that the library behind the McKees was designed by Sir Christopher Wren. Sir Wren was a famous architect who rebuilt St. Paul's Cathedral in London after it was destroyed by a fire in 1666.

Students who go to Cambridge usually live near the university and get around on bicycles. Often in the evening, young men wear suits and girls wear dresses or long skirts, because formal dinners are served in their colleges.

On weekends Mr. Mc-Kee works in the yard. Peter helps him mow the lawn. The hedge needs trimming, and the hanging baskets of flowers along the garage wall have to be watered. The family's house is modern, but 100 years ago the garage was a butcher's shop.

The McKee's dog, Bramble, is part of the family. Like all terriers, Bramble loves to chase chickens. One day he broke through the hedge and got into the local policeman's yard, where he kept his chickens. The policeman brought the dog back and told the McKees that according to the village rules, he could shoot the dog for chasing his chickens. The trouble was, the policeman liked Bramble. Instead of a gun, the policeman brought two posts and some wire to chain the dog up. The family decided that Bramble would hate that, so they put up a big fence around the yard. When they finally finished the project, they all decided it would have been a lot easier to fence in the policeman's chickens.

Alastair plays the saxophone in his school band and in a local jazz band. Sometimes on Saturdays he goes to London with his friends. London is the capital of England and one of the largest cities in the world. Alastair and his friends catch the train from Steeple Mordern. During the week the train goes fast, because people are commuting to work. On weekends the trip takes longer, because the train stops in many towns and villages.

Alastair and his friends like to go to Oxford Street, where there are lots of shops. They often buy cassette tapes of their favorite music, and they enjoy looking at the fashionable clothes. The boys take a bus. They think it is fun to go around the traffic circle called Piccadilly Circus, past Buckingham Palace, where the Queen of England lives, and on to Parliament Square. They check the time on their watches against the big clock tower there before making their way back home. The name of the bell that tolls the hour in the tower is "Big Ben."

17

Mrs. McKee sometimes arranges flowers in the village church. She does it on Saturdays so they are fresh for the services on Sunday morning. The ladies in the village take turns doing them. Most of the women grow the flowers in their gardens.

Thomas goes to Sunday school with his mother, since she is one of the teachers. English people can belong to any religious group, but, like the McKees, many people choose to belong to the Church of England. The Church of England was formed over 350 years ago by King Henry VIII. The service is too long for children, so Mrs. McKee usually reads them a story, and they play games before they join the adults.

Each summer the family takes a vacation in Bosham, which is a sailing village on the south coast of England. They stay with Mrs. McKee's parents. Before he retired, the children's grandfather, Mr. Tibbitts, was an architect. He designed many of the modern houses in the village. Mr. McKee's sister also comes to Bosham for a vacation. Since the house is full, she usually stays at a bed-and-breakfast place in the village and joins the family during the day. A bed-and-breakfast place is a lodging, often in a private home, which is inexpensive and provides breakfast as well as a room. The family celebrates their first day together with a traditional dinner of roast lamb with mint sauce, roast potatoes, cauliflower, carrots, and gravy. For dessert they have fruit salad and homemade meringues.

Mr. Tibbitts takes good care of his garden. Roses grow especially well in England's mild, damp climate. To keep the plants healthy, he cuts off the dead blooms with a pair of pruning shears, or *secateurs*.

The boys love coming down to Bosham, because the family owns two sailboats. Alastair has a boat that he races in the village *regatta*, or race. This year he is teaching Peter to sail.

Before learning to sail the boat himself, Peter helps Alastair. Some of the races take place in nearby Chichester harbor, where there are lots of boats. Mr. and Mrs. McKee like to sail also. Instead of racing, they prefer to sail to a beach where they can have a picnic.

Thomas often meets one of his friends, and they build sand castles. The long beaches have wooden breakwaters to keep the sand from being washed away by the tide. Further along the coast, *groins*, or walls of stone and metal, have been built to break the waves, which wear away the cliffs.

On Wednesdays, Thomas goes with his grandmother to the egg farm in Bosham to buy fresh brown eggs. They can pick out the ones they want. Although there are supermarkets in the towns, people often prefer to buy fresh produce from small shops. They get to know the people serving them, and shopping becomes a social occasion.

The family enjoys tea in the afternoon, and they sit outside for tea whenever possible. Afternoon tea—usually served at about 4:00 P.M.—is an old English tradition. In addition to drinking tea, people eat cookies, cakes, and sometimes sandwiches or a meal. Mrs. McKee remembers a time when they had a French student staying with them. The girl thought the English were crazy, because even when the weather got chilly, tea was still served in the yard—and everyone wrapped blankets around their knees.

After sailing, Peter and Alastair have to roll up the
sails and pack up the boat. While they work, they dis-
cuss racing tactics.

Their father and grandfather sometimes go to the local pub, called the Anchor Bleu, which opens at 6:00 P.M. Here they can talk and relax before the evening meal. The Anchor Bleu is where the boys' mother and father first met. Their mother was with someone else when Mr. McKee walked in. He accidentally stepped on her toes, and then he introduced himself. Their grandmother decorated the top of their parent's wedding cake with a blue anchor in celebration of the place where they met.

After his summer vacation, Peter will start at his new school. He hopes that by next year he will be able to sail by himself so that he can sail in the village race.

The English Language

More than 450 million people in the world speak the English language. Over 1,500 years ago, Germanic tribes called Angles and Saxons settled in what is now England and named it Angle-land. Since then, French, Latin, Greek, Spanish, and Italian are just some of the languages that have contributed words to the English vocabulary. English now has the largest vocabulary of any language in the world.

There are many differences between English as it is spoken in England and English as it is spoken in the United States. Some differences are just changes in spelling or pronunciation, but over time some words or sentences have also altered their structure or meaning.

There are also regional and class differences in the way English people talk. Upper-class English, for example, is distinct from the speech of most ordinary people in England.

Here are some different British and United States words that mean the same thing:

British	U.S.	British	U.S.
biscuit	cookie	joint	roast (meat)
bonnet	hood (car)	jug	pitcher
boot	trunk (car)	lift	elevator
bottles of fruit	cans of fruit	loo	bathroom
car park	parking lot	petrol	gasoline
chemist's shop	drugstore	pram	baby stroller
chips	french fries	public school	private school
crisps	potato chips	puncture	flat tire
face flannel	washcloth	queue	stand in line
flat	apartment	secateurs	pruning shears
football	soccer	take it in turns	take turns
garden	yard	wellingtons	rubber boots
holiday	vacation		

Facts about England

Capital: London

Language: English

Form of Money: pound

Area: 50,363 square miles
(130,439 square kilometers)
    England is a little smaller than the state of New York.

Population: About 46.3 million
    England has almost three times as many people as
    the state of New York.

National Holidays: Bank holidays are days when
all banks are closed. These include: Easter Monday,
Whit Sunday (the seventh Sunday after Easter),
Monday in Whitsun Week, and the first Monday
in August. Boxing Day is also a national holiday.
It is the day after Christmas, when the gentry,
or noblemen, used to box up gifts for their servants.

NORTH
AMERICA

SOUTH
AMERICA

gland

EUROPE

A S I A

AFRICA

AUSTRALIA

Families the World Over

Some children in foreign countries live like you do. Others live very differently. In these books, you can meet children from all over the world. You'll learn about their games and schools, their families and friends, and what it's like to grow up in a faraway land.

Lerner Publications Company, 241 First Avenue North, Minneapolis, Minnesota 55401